This Book Belongs To

Mom.
love?
Cheri

MOTHERS

A Tribute

Ariel Books

Andrews and McMeel

Kansas City

For information write Andrews and McMeel,
a Universal Press Syndicate Company,
4900 Main Street,
Kansas City, Missouri 64112.
10 9
ISBN: 0-8362-3008-6

Library of Congress Catalog Card Number:
91-77101

Book design by Judith A. Stagnitto

Paintings by Frank W. Benson, Mary Cassatt,
Pierre-Auguste Renoir, James Jebusa Shannon and
Elisabeth Vignée-Lebrun.

Mothers must be angels on earth, always at hand to doctor scraped knees, boost dampened spirits, and guide us through the minor setbacks in life. They must be models of inspiration, patient counselors, and sterling examples. They must be everything to everybody.

As children age, they begin to realize the value of a mother's love and the enormous depth of her commitment. No relationship we form can ever be as close or profound.

Here, inspired insights and poems, illuminated with well-known paintings, reflect the grace and beauty of mothers and provide a heartfelt expression of gratitude and love for the most important person in our life.

Quotations

Mother is the name for God in the lips and hearts of children.

—WILLIAM MAKEPEACE THACKERAY

Every mother is like Moses. She does not enter the promised land. She prepares a world she will not see.

—POPE PAUL VI

MOTHERS

All women become like their mothers.
That is their tragedy. No man does.
That's his.

—OSCAR WILDE

Only a mother knows a mother's fondness.

—LADY MARY WORTLEY MONTAGU

A Tribute

You don't have to deserve your mother's
love. You have to deserve your father's.
He's more particular.

—ROBERT FROST

The mother's heart is the child's
schoolroom.

—HENRY WARD BEECHER

MOTHERS

The heart of a mother is a deep abyss at the bottom of which you will always discover forgiveness.

—HONORÉ DE BALZAC

Mothers . . . are the first book read and the last put aside in every child's library.

—C. LENOX REMOND

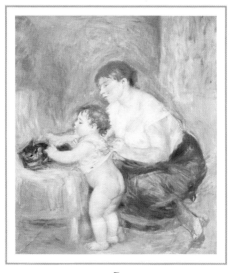

MOTHERS

A mother is not a person to lean on but a person to make leaning unnecessary.

—DOROTHY CANFIELD FISHER

Women as the guardians of children possess a great power. They are the molders of their children's personalities and the arbiters of their development.

—ANN OAKLEY

A Tribute

A mother who is really a mother is never free.

—Honoré de Balzac

Who takes the child by the hand takes the mother by the heart.

—Danish Proverb

MOTHERS

A mother has, perhaps, the hardest earthly
lot; and yet no mother worthy of the name
ever gave herself thoroughly for her child
who did not feel that, after all, she reaped
what she had sown.

—HENRY WARD BEECHER

A Tribute

"She broke the bread into two fragments
and gave them to the children, who ate
with avidity.

'She hath kept none for herself,'
grumbled the Sergeant.

'Because she is not hungry,' said a
soldier.

'Because she is a mother,' said the
Sergeant.''

—VICTOR HUGO

MOTHERS

There is no slave out of heaven like a
loving woman; and of all loving women,
there is no such slave as a mother.

—HENRY WARD BEECHER

The precursor of the mirror is the mother's
face.

—D. W. WINNICOTT

MOTHERS

God could not be everywhere and therefore he made mothers.

—JEWISH PROVERB

My mother was the source from which I derived the guiding principles of my life.

—JOHN WESLEY

A Tribute

I looked on child rearing not only as a
work of love and duty but as a profession
that was fully as interesting and challenging
as any honorable profession in the world
and one that demanded the best that I could
bring to it.

—ROSE KENNEDY

MOTHERS

What the mother sings to the cradle goes all
the way down to the coffin.

—HENRY WARD BEECHER

A man who has been the indisputable
favourite of his mother keeps for life the
feeling of a conqueror, that confidence of
success that often induces real success.

—SIGMUND FREUD

A Tribute

The hand that rocks the cradle is the hand
that rules the world.

—W. S. ROSS

Where there is a mother in the house,
matters speed well.

—AMOS BRONSON ALCOTT

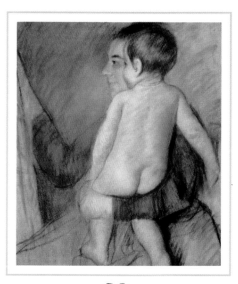

A Tribute

In the man whose childhood has known caresses, there is always a fibre of memory that can be touched to gentle issues.

—GEORGE ELIOT

Of all the rights of women, the greatest is to be a mother.

—LIN YUTANG

MOTHERS

In general those parents have the most reverence who deserve it.

—SAMUEL JOHNSON

Men are what their mothers made them.

—RALPH WALDO EMERSON

A Tribute

Every beetle is a gazelle in the eyes of its mother.

—MOORISH PROVERB

There is so much to teach, and the time goes so fast.

—ERMA BOMBECK

MOTHERS

I really learned it all from mothers.

—DR. SPOCK

It's not easy being a mother. If it were
fathers would do it.

—DOROTHY, "THE GOLDEN GIRLS"

MOTHERS

Let France have good mothers, and she will have good sons.

—NAPOLEON BONAPARTE

Because I am a mother, I am capable of being shocked: as I never was when I was not one.

—MARGARET ATWOOD

A Tribute

There's a lot more to being a woman than
being a mother. But there's a lot more to
being a mother than most people suspect.

—ROSEANNE BARR

Mother's love grows by giving.

—CHARLES LAMB

MOTHERS

Children are the anchors that hold a mother
to life.

—SOPHOCLES

I never thought that you should be
rewarded for the greatest privilege of life.

—MARY ROPER COKER, ON BEING CHOSEN
"MOTHER OF THE YEAR," 1958.

A Tribute

A mother's arms are made of tenderness
and children sleep soundly in them.

—Victor Hugo

For me, a line from my mother is more
efficacious than all the homilies preached in
Lent.

—Henry Wadsworth Longfellow

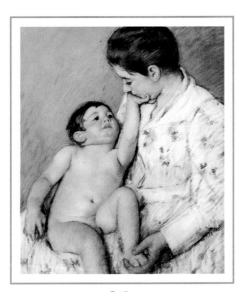

A Tribute

When God thought of Mother, he must
have laughed with satisfaction, and framed
it quickly—so rich, so deep, so divine, so
full of soul, power, and beauty, was the
conception.

—HENRY WARD BEECHER

MOTHERS

With animals you don't see males caring for the offspring. It's against nature. It's a woman's prerogative and duty, and a privilege.

—PRINCESS GRACE OF MONACO

A Tribute

This is the reason why mothers are more devoted to their children than fathers: it is that they suffer more in giving them birth and are more certain that they are their own.

—ARISTOTLE

MOTHERS

——————

All that I am or hope to be I owe to my angel mother. I remember my mother's prayers and they have always followed me. They have clung to me all my life.

—ABRAHAM LINCOLN

A Tribute

A mother is the truest friend we have,
when trials, heavy and sudden, fall upon
us; when adversity takes the place of
prosperity; when friends who rejoice with
us in our sunshine, desert us when troubles
thicken around us, still will she cling to us,
and endeavor by her kind precepts and
counsels to dissipate the clouds of darkness,
and cause peace to return to our hearts.

—WASHINGTON IRVING

MOTHERS

My mother was the most beautiful woman I ever saw. All I am I owe to my mother. I attribute all my success in life to the moral, intellectual, and physical education I received from her.

—GEORGE WASHINGTON

MOTHERS

Children are what the mothers are.

—WALTER SAVAGE LANDOR

A kiss from my mother made me a painter.

—BENJAMIN WEST

I would desire for a friend the son who
never resisted the tears of his mother.

—LACRETALLE

A Tribute

In all my efforts to learn to read, my
mother shared fully my ambition and
sympathized with me and aided me in
every way she could. If I have done
anything in life worth attention, I feel sure
that I inherited the disposition from my
mother.

—Booker T. Washington

MOTHERS

My mother had a slender, small body, but a large heart—a heart so large that everybody's grief and everybody's joy found welcome in it, and hospitable accommodation.

—MARK TWAIN

MOTHERS

Mother—that was the bank where we deposited all our hurts and worries.

—T. DeWitt Talmage

There is a religion in all deep love, but the love of a mother is the veil of a softer light between the heart and the heavenly Father.

—Samuel Taylor Coleridge

A Tribute

The mother loves her child most divinely,
not when she surrounds him with comfort
and anticipates his wants, but when she
resolutely holds him to the highest
standards and is content with nothing less
than his best.

—HAMILTON WRIGHT MABIE

MOTHERS

Some are kissing mothers and some are scolding mothers, but it is love just the same, and most mothers kiss and scold together.

—PEARL S. BUCK

What are Raphael's Madonnas but the shadow of a mother's love, fixed in permanent outline forever?

—THOMAS WENTWORTH HIGGINSON

—

A Tribute

The most powerful ties are the ones to the people who gave birth to us . . . it hardly seems to matter how many years have passed, how many betrayals there may have been, how much misery in the family; we remain connected, even against our wills.

—ANTHONY BRANDT

Poetry

There was a place in childhood, that I
  remember well,
And there a voice of sweetest tone, bright
  fairy tales did tell,
And gentle words, and fond embrace, were
  given with joy to me,
When I was in that happy place upon my
  mother's knee.

—Samuel Lover

MOTHERS

Sonnets are full of love, and this my tome
Has many sonnets: so here now shall be
One sonnet more, a loving sonnet from me
To her whose heart is my heart's quiet
    home,
To my first Love, my Mother on whose
    knee
I learnt love-lore that is not troublesome:
Whose service is my special dignity
And she my lodestar while I go and come.

—

A Tribute

And so because you love, and because
I love you, Mother, I have woven a wreath
Of rhymes wherewith to crown your
    honored name:
In you not fourscore years can dim the
    flame
Of love, whose blessed glow transcends the
    laws
Of time and change and mortal life and
    death.

—CHRISTINA G. ROSSETTI

MOTHERS

You painted no Madonnas
On chapel walls in Rome;
But with a touch diviner
You lived one in your home.
You wrote no lofty poems
That critics counted art;
But with a nobler vision,
You lived them in your heart.

You carved no shapeless marble
To some high soul design

A Tribute

But with a finer sculpture
You shaped this soul of mine.
You built no great cathedrals
That centuries applaud;
But with a grace exquisite
Your life cathedraled God.
Had I the gift of Raphael
Or Michelangelo
O what a rare Madonna
My mother's life would show.

—THOMAS FESSENDEN

MOTHERS

I thought a child was given to sanctify
A woman, set her in the sight of all
The clear-eyed heavens, a chosen minister
To do their business, and lead spirits up
The difficult blue heights. A woman lives
Not bettered, quickened toward the truth
  and good
Through being a mother?—then she's
  none.

—ELIZABETH BARRETT BROWNING

MOTHERS

So for the mother's sake the child was dear,
And dearer was the mother for the child.

—SAMUEL TAYLOR COLERIDGE

My mother was as mild as any saint,
And nearly canonized by all she knew,
So gracious was her tact and tenderness.

—ALFRED, LORD TENNYSON

A Tribute

There is none,
In all this cold and hollow world, no fount
Of deep, strong, deathless love, save that
   within
A mother's heart.

—FELICIA HEMANS

Years to a mother bring distress
But do not make her love the less.

—WILLIAM WORDSWORTH

MOTHERS

Hundreds of stars in the pretty sky,
Hundreds of shells on the shore together,
Hundreds of birds that go singing by,
Hundreds of birds in the sunny weather,
Hundreds of dewdrops to greet the dawn,
Hundreds of bees in the purple clover,
Hundreds of butterflies on the lawn,
But only *one mother* the wide world over.

—GEORGE COOPER

A Tribute

They say that man is mighty;
He governs land and sea,
He wields a mighty scepter
O'er lesser powers that be.
But a mightier power and stronger
Man from his throne has hurled,
For the hand that rocks the cradle
Is the hand that rules the world.

—WILLIAM ROSS WALLACE

A Tribute

A picture memory brings to me:
I look across the year and see
Myself beside my mother's knee.

I feel her gentle hand restrain
My selfish moods, and know again
A child's blind sense of wrong and pain.

But wiser now, a man gray grown,
My childhood's needs are better known,
My mother's chastening love I own.

—JOHN GREENLEAF WHITTIER

MOTHERS

My Blessed Mother dozing in her chair
On Christmas Day seemed an embodied
   Love,
A comfortable Love with soft brown hair
Softened and silvered to a tint of dove;
A better sort of Venus with an air
Angelical from thoughts that dwell above;
A wiser Pallas in whose body fair
Enshrined a blessed soul looks out thereof.
Winter brought holly then; now Spring has
   brought
Paler and frailer snowdrops shivering;

A Tribute

And I have brought a simple humble
   thought—
I her devoted duteous Valentine—
A lifelong thought which drills this song I
   sing.
A lifelong love to this dear saint of mine.

—CHRISTINA G. ROSSETTI

MOTHERS

Over my heart, in the days that are flown,
No love like mother-love ever has shone;
No other worship abides and endures—
Faithful, unselfish, and patient like yours:
None like a mother can charm away pain,
Long I to-night for your presence again.
Come from the silence so long and so
   deep;—
Rock me to sleep, Mother—rock me to
   sleep!

—ELIZABETH AKERS ALLEN

MOTHERS

A mother's love is the golden link
Binding youth to age;
And he is still but a child,
However time may have furrowed his
   cheek,
Who cannot happily recall, with a softened
   heart,
The fond devotion and gentle chidings
Of the best friend God ever gave.

—CHRISTIAN BOVÉE

A Tribute

A woman's love
Is mighty, but a mother's heart is weak,
And by its weakness overcomes.

—JAMES RUSSELL LOWELL

MOTHERS

From THE CHILDREN'S HOUR

A whisper, and then a silence:
Yet I know by their merry eyes
They are plotting and planning together
To take me by surprise.

A sudden rush from the stairway,
A sudden raid from the hall!
By three doors left unguarded
They enter my castle wall!

A Tribute

They climb up into my turret
O'er the arms and back of my chair;
If I try to escape, they surround me;
They seem to be everywhere.

They almost devour me with kisses,
Their arms about me entwine.
Till I think of the Bishop of Bingen
In his Mouse-Tower on the Rhine!

I have you fast in my fortress,
And will not let you depart,

MOTHERS

But put you down into the dungeon
In the round-tower of my heart.

And there will I keep you forever,
Yes, forever and a day,
Till the wall shall crumble to ruin,
And moulder in dust away.

—HENRY WADSWORTH LONGFELLOW

A Tribute

The light upon his eyelids pricked them
  wide
And staring out at us with their all blue,
As half perplexed between the angelhood
He had been away to visit in his sleep,
And our most mortal presence, gradually
He saw his mother's face, accepting it
In change for heaven itself with such a
  smile
As might have well been learnt there.

—Elizabeth Barrett Browning

MOTHERS

In the heavens above,

The angels, whispering to one another,

Can find, among their burning terms of
   love,

None so devotional as that of "Mother."

—EDGAR ALLAN POE